P9-DTE-781

Published in 2020 by Groundwood Books / House of Anansi Press
groundwoodbooks.com
Second printing 2022

We gratefully acknowledge for their financial support of our publishing
program the Canada Council for the Arts, the Ontario Arts Council and the
Government of Canada.

Canada Council   Conseil des Arts
for the Arts   du Canada

ONTARIO ARTS COUNCIL
CONSEIL DES ARTS DE L'ONTARIO
an Ontario government agency
un organisme du gouvernement de l'Ontario

With the participation of the Government of Canada
Avec la participation du gouvernement du Canada | Canadä

Library and Archives Canada Cataloguing in Publication
Title: If you want to visit a sea garden / by Kay Weisman ; illustrated by Roy
Henry Vickers.
Names: Weisman, Kay, author. | Vickers, Roy Henry, illustrator.
Identifiers: Canadiana (print) 20190225548 | Canadiana (ebook) 20190227087
| ISBN 9781554989706 (hardcover) | ISBN 9781554989713 (EPUB) | ISBN
9781773064291 (Kindle)
Subjects: LCSH: Mollusk culture — Northwest, Pacific — Juvenile literature.
| LCSH: Clams — Northwest, Pacific — Juvenile literature. | LCSH: Indians of
North America — Food — Northwest, Pacific — Juvenile literature.
Classification: LCC SH373 .W45 2020 | DDC j639/.44091643—dc23

The illustrations were created digitally.
Design by Michael Solomon
Printed and bound in Canada

If You Want to Visit a Sea Garden

by Kay Weisman

illustrated by Roy Henry Vickers

 GROUNDWOOD BOOKS
HOUSE OF ANANSI PRESS
TORONTO / BERKELEY

To Kwaxsistalla Wathl'thla Clan Chief Adam Dick, who first explained sea gardens to the rest of us, and to all sea gardeners past, present and future.

— KW

It is a joy and an honor to work on this book with Kay Weisman at a time when we are giving more credence to the Indigenous nations of Canada. It is important to learn how nations lived for thousands of years in harmony with nature. I dedicate my work as an artist here to the ancestors who passed down their wealth of knowledge and artistic expression.

— RHV

If you want to visit a sea garden ...

... you'll have to get up really early. These magical gardens only reveal themselves at the lowest tides. In the summer months those often happen at the break of day.

Hop into the boat, and zip up your life jacket.
Do you see the watermarks along the shore left by the last
high tide?

We'll anchor in a safe place. The tide will rise while we're here, and we don't want our boat to float away.

Listen closely for the symphony of clams, welcoming us to their beach. Here, there and everywhere they spurt and sputter, exhaling right on cue.

Step carefully so you don't slip on the rocks. Many of them are covered with barnacles — tiny creatures that live inside sharp shells.

Stroll to the edge of the water to look at the reef up close. For thousands of years the First Peoples have constructed these architectural wonders. Some reefs have been built all at once. Others have developed over time, as people clear boulders while digging for clams. But both do their job, creating a healthy habitat for sea life.

If you perch near the top of the wall, you can see the creatures on both sides. Whelks and sea cucumbers, fish fry and kelp, sea stars and bat stars, hermit crabs and rock crabs, chitons, barnacles and octopuses all make their homes on this beach.

Look at the squirting holes that announce, "Clams live here!" Butter clams, littlenecks and cockles thrive just beneath the beach under our feet. The warm, food-filled waters inside the wall are just right for growing healthy clams.

Imagine the generations of First Peoples who have maintained this wall in order to feed their families. They have come here to build and care for the sea garden, harvest and eat clams, and share stories and knowledge about this special place.

Don't forget to dig for clams! You can use a yew stick, fork or shovel to collect these tasty mollusks. We can steam some to eat now or string them up to smoke for later.

We'll need to tend our garden before we leave. Can you help me roll this stray boulder down to the wall? I'll break up the empty clamshells, and we can gently rake them into the beach. Then we can clear away the driftwood and seaweed. All of these things will give new clams room to grow.

You'll be surprised how quickly the tide changes, submerging the reef again. We can no longer see it, but the wall is still at work, creating a habitat for all these creatures.

If you want to visit a sea garden ...
... you'll have to get up really early,
but it will be worth it.

MORE ABOUT SEA GARDENS

Sea gardens, also known as clam gardens, have been found all along the Pacific Northwest coast, from Puget Sound in Washington State through British Columbia and northward to Alaska. Indigenous peoples have their own names for these special places. The term "sea garden" is used here because these sites are home to many kinds of edible marine life in addition to clams.

These human-constructed reefs are composed of boulders lined up at the lowest tide line, and often stretch between outcroppings of bedrock. The walls range from just a few feet (less than 1 m) to nearly a mile (1.6 km) in length, and many stand about 3 feet (1 m) high. Archeologists have determined that some of these walls are at least 3,500 years old.

Since their construction, managed sea gardens have provided the peoples of the Northwest Coast with a dependable source of food. Clams, in particular, are a rich source of lean protein, iron and vitamins, and are readily available year round, although many sea gardens have fallen into disuse in recent years.

Scientists studying sea gardens have confirmed that much traditional Indigenous knowledge about these reefs also mirrors best scientific practice. Ecologists have determined that a gently sloped sea garden can yield up to four times the number of butter clams and more than twice as many littleneck clams as a similarly sized, unmodified beach. Moreover, clams in sea gardens grow faster than their counterparts in non-walled beaches — especially when larger clams are harvested regularly, providing smaller clams with additional growing space. Clearly, coastal peoples have a long history as successful sustainable-resource managers.

Additionally, sea gardens have always been places of learning. Extended families and communities gather at these sites to harvest and eat clams, and to transfer information. Here traditional knowledge holders share ideas about managing resources, their cultural norms and worldview, and the importance of family.

To acknowledge the significance of sea gardens to the food security of Indigenous peoples, First Nations and other partners are currently refurbishing several reefs along British Columbia's coast. It is hoped that these beaches can once again become places of learning — for all who wish to understand their secrets.

To find out more about sea gardens visit the Clam Garden Network website at clamgarden.com.

Acknowledgments

Special thanks to
- Members of the Clam Garden Network — especially Skye Augustine, Nicole Smith and Dana Lepofsky — for allowing me to visit several amazing sea gardens and for their help in checking this manuscript. Any errors are my own.
- Audrey Dallimore, NSERC, Hakai Institute, Gulf Islands National Park Reserve and Bamfield Marine Sciences Centre for travel assistance and logistical support.
- Kwaxsistalla Wathl'thla Clan Chief Adam Dick for reviewing this manuscript. — KW

Thanks to Cyril Aster, Kitkatla, BC, for his reference photos. — RHV

Photos above (from left to right):

An aerial view of a sea garden near the northern end of Vancouver Island. Courtesy of Mary Morris.

Members of the Clam Garden Restoration Project tend a sea garden on Saltspring Island, British Columbia. © Parks Canada / Allison Stocks.

Scientists on Quadra Island, British Columbia, gather information on how well marine animals grow in sea gardens. Courtesy of Dana Lepofsky.